D1194557

INTRODUCTION

It is now some thirty years since steam disappeared from regular use on the lines of Southern England. During that time a radical change has taken place with perhaps a more efficient railway resulting (ask the commuters if they agree!), but one which lacks the variety of years past, when different engines hauled trains of different lengths, and the same service on two consecutive days would reveal a different make-up and different type of engine at its head.

To those who did not witness the years before the mid-1960s it is perhaps hard to imagine the change that has taken place; the only record is available through the lenses of cameras that were pointed at the trains and engines around the area. Eastleigh was a railway town for many years, so almost everyone worked 'inside', as it was referred to; upon meeting someone it was not a question of where do you work, but in which shop or depot.

Of the vast majority of locomotive enthusiasts who visited the scene few may have come on more than a handful of occasions, there being so many other worthy locations to attend – Swindon, Doncaster and Crewe to name only three. One exception to this was Walter (Wally) Gilburt. Wally, who lived near Fareham, was a regular visitor to Eastleigh, and fortunately several times a year, often several times a month, would point his camera at engines in the shed, the works and its environs, with the result that a true record is at last available of the variety of different engines seen at Eastleigh, mainly between 1947 and 1962.

To start with, Wally photographed machines long overdue for repair, old designs retained because of the requirements of war, as well as numerous engines visiting to have the insignia of their new owners 'British Railways' affixed. Later, newer designs are apparent, each again of distinctive type and again faithfully recorded by Wally. To provide some variety there is also a glimpse of a few other Southern locations visited by him, again the subjects to be recorded were varied in the extreme.

Much of his work is seen here for the first time. Taken in the main on large format negatives, the views deserve an airing, especially as composition and quality were paramount. (The bracketed numbers after some of the captions are Wally's reference numbers.)

Journey back then fifty years to Eastleigh and the Southern, a time of petrol rationing when the railway was still the prime mover for passengers and freight. Today so much of what we have is taken for granted – one example, perhaps, being this text, typed on computer and somewhat incongruous when dealing with the subject of the steam engine.

Kevin Robertson

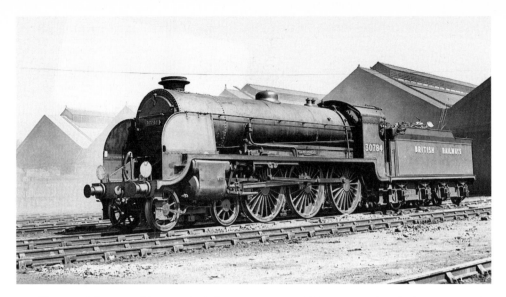

I could not resist this view of 'King Arthur' class 4–6–0 no. 30784 'Sir Nerovens' as the first picture in the book. The atmosphere of smoke and steam emanating from the shed was, I feel, so typical of the area for many years. How the families living in the railway cottages in nearby Campbell Road ever successfully dried their washing outside I can only guess! 30784 itself is depicted in a form of transitory livery, malachite green – including partly on the smoke deflectors and yet with British Railways insignia on the tender. The engine was built in August 1925 and lasted until October 1959; the photograph was taken on 12 June 1949. (215)

Away from the shed, temporarily, and to the nearby station at Eastleigh where waiting passengers pause to watch as 35017 'Belgian Marine' passes with the down 'Bournemouth Belle' working on 9 April 1949. This luxury all Pullman train ran between Waterloo and Bournemouth once each way daily and was available to passengers on payment of a supplementary fare. The train called only at Southampton *en route*, and the journey time was in the order of two hours. (28)

Seen from a slightly earlier perspective and with the same working passing the large Eastleigh East signal-box. The engine is an unidentified member of the same 'Merchant Navy' class. Eastleigh East box was at the north end of the station and yet was named East because route-wise this was the east end of the station to London and the signal-boxes were named accordingly. Points of the compass were important at the time, even if not true magnetic north! Two other signal-boxes operated the station as well: Eastleigh West, to control the Portsmouth line and exit from the engine shed and works, and Eastleigh South on the Portsmouth line itself. Nowadays a single panel box stands on the opposite side of the line to the old structure, and the progress of trains is witnessed by coloured lights on a panel.

On 10 April 1948 Wally recorded 'Lord Nelson' class 4–6–0, no. 862 'Lord Collingwood' at the head of what may only be described as a Bournemouth line working. The picture was taken from the end of the up platform at the station and with the Bishopstoke Road bridge casting the shadow across the tracks. As an aside, the name Collingwood was the middle name of the redoubtable Stephen Townroe. When the engine was withdrawn he acquired one of the name-plates and for many years it stood in the porchway of his Hampshire home.

Passing through the station on the down through line is another 'Lord Nelson', this time no. 30864 'Sir Martin Frobisher' and with evidence of hard work in the form of the burns at the bottom of the smokebox door. Designed by R.E.L. Maunsell, the stock would also appear to be of his origin as well. Although Wally was usually meticulous with his records of dates and locations of his photographs there are some gaps, of which this is one, although it is reasonable to surmise the period is around 1948/9.

A not unusual visitor to Eastleigh on 12 April 1947 was former Ministry of Supply 2–8–0 no. 77098, no doubt in for repair from its well-worn and travelled appearance. Hundreds of these and the slightly larger 2–10–0 variant were built to assist in the war effort, with the vast majority working overseas. No. 77098 has probably returned from a similar assignment: witness the air pump alongside the smokebox. Later several hundred were taken over by British Railways and numbered in the 90xxx series, working primarily in the Midlands and North. (2)

BRITAIN'S RAILWAYS IN OLD PHOTOGRAPHS

STEAM AROUND EASTLEIGH

KEVIN ROBERTSON

The
History
Press

First published in 1997
This edition first published in 2009

The History Press
The Mill, Brimscombe Port
Stroud, Gloucestershire, GL5 2QG
www.thehistorypress.co.uk

© Kevin Robertson, 1997, 2009

The right of Kevin Robertson to be identified as the Author
of this work has been asserted in accordance with the
Copyrights, Designs and Patents Act 1988.

All rights reserved. No part of this book may be reprinted
or reproduced or utilised in any form or by any electronic,
mechanical or other means, now known or hereafter invented,
including photocopying and recording, or in any information
storage or retrieval system, without the permission in writing
from the Publishers.
British Library Cataloguing in Publication Data.
A catalogue record for this book is available from the British Library.

ISBN 978 0 7524 5035 3

Typesetting and origination by The History Press
Printed in Great Britain

A particularly interesting photograph of Porter-built USA tank No. WD1261 outside the works at Eastleigh sometime after September 1947. This engine was similar but not identical in design to the Vulcan-built examples of the same class, of which a total of thirteen were purchased by the Southern Railway primarily for shunting in Southampton Docks. One Porter-built example, no. 61 (later 30061), was also retained. No. 1261, though, was acquired purely as a source of spare parts and was subsequently cannibalised. The photograph is one of few to show the machine in its complete state.

Known as 'Large Hoppers', the forty members of the 'L11' class dated from 1903 and although the example depicted here, no. 134, carried the lowest number of the class it was not the first to be built. At the time Wally recorded it at Eastleigh on 12 April 1947 the engine was already some forty-three years old and presents a somewhat Victorian appearance, accentuated perhaps by the tall chimney. The class were widespread throughout the former Western Section and could be seen in varied roles, such as local passenger/goods workings to excursion traffic. No. 134 is seen apparently fresh from a repaint – probably the last it had, for the engine was withdrawn in February 1951, by which time it carried the BR identification of 30134. It was later scrapped at Eastleigh. (3)

From 1946 onwards the railways of the country were persuaded by the government to adopt oil fuel as an alternative to coal and consequently a number of engines were converted. Among these were eight members of the 'L11' class; the original intention had been to convert fifteen, although the whole scheme was later curtailed amid considerable embarrassment within Whitehall. Records indicate no. 148 was so dealt with in September 1947, and the photograph was taken shortly after this time but before the addition of electric lighting in November of the same year. In its modified guise no. 148 worked from Eastleigh, and like other converted machines was popular with the crews. The use of oil as a fuel came to an abrupt end in late September 1948 and the engine was laid aside for some time, although not officially withdrawn until March 1952. Presumably it was subsequently towed away from the Hampshire town, for according to Don Bradley cutting up was undertaken at Ashford. (24)

Another oil-burning 'L11', this time no. 437, and seen in somewhat grimy condition outside Eastleigh shed. The electric lights referred to in the previous caption, which were added to all the oil burners, have been fitted, while dominant in the view is the welded oil tank affixed to the top of the tender. Upon subsequent withdrawal the generators used to provide power for the electric lighting were removed and utilised on USA tanks working at Southampton Docks. Here they found a new lease of life affording power for radio communication.

There were ten members of the big 'D15' class, of which no. 463 was the doyenne, dating back to February 1912. Intended for front line passenger services, the class was quickly provided with superheating by Robert Urie and continued to afford sterling service until trains' weights and speeds dictated a need for even larger engines in about 1925/6. In consequence the class was transferred to Portsmouth line duties and in so doing lost their eight-wheeled tenders; these were replaced by the six-wheeled variant seen here. As an oil burner no. 463 was well liked, and worked Bournemouth, Salisbury and Portsmouth services. It was laid aside in October 1948 and never ran again before withdrawal in December 1951. The total recorded mileage in its lifetime was nearly 1.4 million miles. (23)

Urie-designed 'King Arthur' class 4–6–0 no. 740 'Merlin' at Eastleigh, probably *c.* 1947. As with the other engines so converted, no. 740 was popular with its crews, and with the firemen especially who were able to sit down throughout journeys. The comfort of passengers in the following train was less likely, for an all-pervading smell of oil resulted, which some said had a mild laxative effect. With the abandonment of the scheme no. 740 was considered too precious to withdraw, and (along with the other four members of the class to be converted) reverted back to coal firing during the autumn of 1948.

A final view of one of the oil burners, no. 752 'Linette' outside Eastleigh shed, 10 April 1948, seen as modified by Bulleid with multiple jet blast pipe and large diameter chimney. The full story of the conversions is given in my book *Leader and Southern Experimental Steam*. Sister engine no. 749 also carried the rather ungainly oil tank featured atop the tender. Apparently the tank itself was slightly loose and could be seen sliding forwards towards the crew when under heavy braking. It was retained sufficiently by bolts before injury or damage could ensue, but nevertheless created more than one anxious moment on the footplate. (41)

Introduced in 1938/9 as the last design by R.E.L. Maunsell before his retirement, the 'Q' class 0–6–0 engines were perhaps typical of a generation of steam engines of similar wheel arrangement. Intended primarily for goods work they also appeared on branch passenger and special workings, although they were disliked by Oliver Bulleid, Maunsell's successor. He is alleged to have remarked that he arrived too late to stop them being built. The engine is seen alongside the coaling stage at Eastleigh on 10 April 1948 sporting clean black paintwork, possibly after a visit to the nearby works. (25)

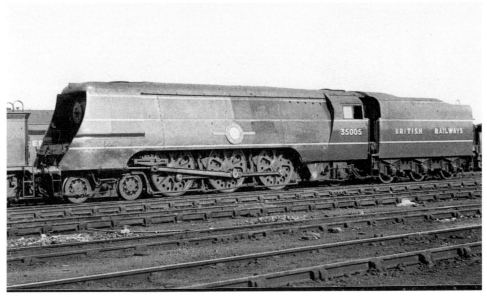

'Merchant Navy' class 4–6–2 no. 35005 'Canadian Pacific' at Eastleigh, 10 April 1948. At this stage the engine is in almost original condition and has yet to receive a wedge-fronted cab. Introduced by Bulleid from 1941 onwards these engines were generally well received by the footplate staff, who for years had battled with ever increasing train weights and often underpowered engines. No members of the class were at the time allocated to Eastleigh, so no. 35005 may have been pending a visit to the nearby works or possibly awaiting a particular special working. (35)

Carrying the temporary identification of s787, this is 'Sir Menadeuke' awaiting its next tour of duty on 10 April 1948. Livery is what appears to be malachite green, including the top half of the smoke deflectors, a vivid contrast to the black of the adjacent smokebox. The then standard wording of 'British Railways' has also been applied to the tender, replacing the word 'Southern'; this was later replaced with what was known as the 'cycling lion' emblem. (36)

A throwback to the nineteenth century in the form of no. 30458 'Ironside', taken over by the LSWR when that railway acquired the Southampton Dock Company in 1891. At that time 'Ironside' and its sister engine 'Clausentum' were just one year old, both destined to see service far from their native haunts – at Poole, Battersea, Fratton and Guildford as well as within the docks themselves. Renumbered as seen in September 1949 it appears also to have been given a repaint, probably its last one for it was retired in June 1954.

Another antique was no. 0334, which had been constructed back in 1876. By 1931, though, only three of the class were left in service, with their time spent either shunting the yards at Eastleigh or occasionally venturing to Southampton Docks. No. 0334 was then laid aside for some five years from mid-1933 before being overhauled and loaned to the Kent & East Sussex Railway for fifteen months before an ignominious return to Eastleigh as part of the formation within a goods train. This time there would be no reprieve and the years 1941 to 1949 were spent languishing in a siding awaiting a call to be turned into razor blades or the like. Such a long wait is in itself of interest, especially in view of the urgent call for scrap of almost every sort at the time. Was there, then, perhaps consideration that such an elderly machine should be reprieved again because of the war effort, or was it just pressure of work that prevented scrapping taking place? No. 3334, as she was then, would surely have been a worthy candidate for preservation, but such thoughts were in their infancy and she survives now only in photographic form.

Returning to the station for a brief while, and 30772 'Sir Percivale' passes by on the through line with an inter-regional working, 9 April 1949. Such services still operate today – and still fail to call at Eastleigh, preference being given to the nearby Southampton Parkway station instead. Aside from the train so much of the contemporary railway scene has altered, for example the magnificent telegraph poles, the board crossings between the tracks and the wooden building on the down platform. (50)

One of the big 'H15' class 4–6–0s passes through Eastleigh on a sunny day in April 1949. Carrying the BR number 30524 together with requisite smokebox plate, the tender still displays 'Southern': has a tender exchange taken place? In the background is part of the carriage works together with the renowned platform tree, a stump of which still survives in 1997. (52)

No. 30752 'Linette' again, this time alongside the down side buildings at Eastleigh, which were swept away during a partial rebuilding in 1966/7. Sadly the replacement structure was a pre-cast concrete affair, austere yet functional, but which has not stood the test of time. The footbridge remains, its design pure LSWR. (49)

Another unlisted photograph depicts Ashford 'N' class 2–6–0 no. 31827 outside the front of the shed, probably *c.* 1949. Originally an SECR design, the 'N' and similar 'U' class were regular performers throughout the Southern system and were popular with crews. No. 31827 ended its days in September 1963 being sold to the Cashmores, scrap merchants at Newport, South Wales. It was probably cut up soon afterwards.

Against the background of a stormy sky, no. 30773 'Sir Lavaine' appears ex-works at Eastleigh, 27 June 1946. As this was the nearest depot to the works, locomotives would arrive at the shed to have their fires dropped before entering the works for repair. Following attention the first trip would be with a works crew after which, and assuming all was in order, the newly repaired machine would return to the nearby shed for the requisite number of running-in turns before final dispatch to its parent shed. (66)

Built as the principal heavy goods design for the LSWR and perpetuated by Maunsell for the Southern Railway, the first twenty engines of the 'S15' class were constructed at Eastleigh in 1920/21. They performed sterling work for over forty years on trains sometimes consisting of as many as seventy vans between Southampton and London; most of the class was shedded at Feltham depot. As such their goods work was principally during the night hours, when they could be heard sure-footedly climbing the long bank north of Eastleigh through Winchester. Daylight saw them pressed into service on relief passenger workings, particularly on summer Saturdays and on such workings as Waterloo to Lymington trains.

Dating back to 1890, William Adams' 'O2' class 0–4–4 tanks are reported as having cost only £1,500 when new. If this were the case then it was a sound investment for several of the class survived well into BR days, with a number transferred on to the Isle of Wight to form the mainstay of motive power on the island right up to the demise of steam in 1966. The mainland versions, which retained the original small bunker seen here, retired earlier, but before this were popular with the crews, being robust and reliable engines. Portrayed in late June 1948 after a repaint, no. 30183 had by April 1950 moved to Plymouth and was still at work in 1960, albeit in a poor state, often to be found on pilot duties at Kings Road, Devonport. It was finally withdrawn in September 1961. (67)

An LBSCR design now, in the form of a rebuilt 'E1' class 0–6–0 dating back to 1878. Considered surplus to requirements in the late 1920s, ten members of the class were modified in the form shown here as class 'E1R', complete with pony truck – thus making them into the 0–6–2T wheel arrangement. In this modified form they were set to work in the West Country, although a number of complaints were received from passengers owing to rough riding which was so severe as to transmit itself to the coaches they hauled. Apparently the crews themselves did not complain; perhaps they were made of sterner stuff. A number of the class were then rebalanced and continued to work passenger duties, although others were relegated to goods and shunting work. As BR no. 32124, and depicted here on 27 June 1948, the engine survived until January 1959, being eighty-one years old when it was finally withdrawn. (68)

No. 34042 'Dorchester' in beautiful external condition and ex-works having just had its cab modified to a 'V' front, 15 April 1949. This change was undertaken in an attempt to improve the forward view available to the crew, although with any large steam design this was necessarily going to be restricted. It would appear the engine has also received a repaint as until the time the photograph was taken the small 's' prefix had been carried. 'Dorchester' was at this time less than three years old and was rebuilt without the air-smooth casing in January 1959. (70)

A brief interlude now at Shawford just a few miles north of Eastleigh, where on 18 April 1948 records show Wally's camera captured nine separate trains. One of these was this 'M7' class tank, no. 48, still in Southern livery and with what was a typical local working of just two coaches and a van. Shawford was the commencement of the four track section to Eastleigh; as no. 48 was signalled to run the 3 miles on the down through road it may be assumed this was a quiet time of day with no express workings due. (99)

Taken on the same day and at the same location was this view of 'T9' no. 120, happily now preserved but on this occasion still earning revenue with what may be a Southampton Terminus train. Both engine and coaches, two three-coach sets, are pure South Western design, and so give an example of the variety to be seen on the railway at this time – as referred to in the introduction. (97)

Also at Shawford but this time on 31 July 1948, 21C12 'United States Line' has charge of the London-bound Bournemouth Belle express, complete with duty number on the smokebox. Such numbers were intended to assist signalmen and others in identifying trains, although with its headboard and all Pullman stock there would be little chance of confusion on this occasion. (118)

Although not apparently within Wally's listings, I felt this view of M7 tank no. 324 at what is probably Guildford is well worthy of inclusion. The odd items of clutter (ranging from the pile of coal, or is it ash, on the far platform, to the corrugated building and signal wire expansion joint) so typical of the period make for an interesting composition. The whole scene is an example of the ad hoc nature of so much of the railway scene, much of which would now be frowned upon by health and safety legislation.

For goods work originally on the lines operated by the LBSCR, seventeen engines of the 'K' class were introduced in batches between 1913 and 1921. Small by comparison with goods designs on other railways, they were adequate for the limited goods available to their former owners and performed sterling work for several decades. A general run-down in facilities at Brighton Works in the 1930s meant that all seventeen were allocated to Eastleigh for necessary repairs, and accordingly no. 32344 is seen fresh from overhaul outside the shed on 10 April 1948. The comparison between clean and dirty engines at Eastleigh was always striking, although it must be said it is doubtful if no. 32344 remained in this condition for very long. Sadly all seventeen of the class were withdrawn in November and December 1962, and were broken up at Eastleigh, Stewarts Lane or Norwich. (110)

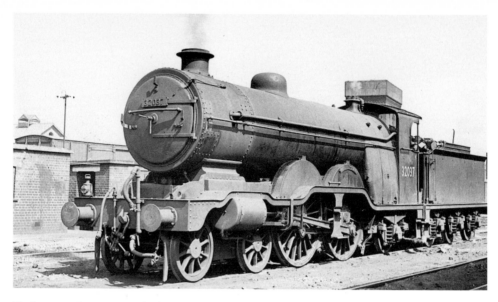

The largest tender engines on the former LBSCR were the Marsh design of 'Atlantics', similar in appearance to a design then operating on the Great Northern Railway. This photograph of no. 32037 'Selsey Bill' was taken on 10 June 1950 at Bricklayers Arms, south London, on which day Wally's records indicate he visited a number of locations, including Stewarts Lane, New Cross Gate, Hither Green, Norwood Junction and Marylebone, taking some thirty-one photographs. For no. 32037 this would be the final full year of service as she was withdrawn in July 1951, although the last of the LBSCR 'Atlantic' design would continue in service until September 1956. (815)

Returning to Eastleigh, and a beautifully clean 'M7' tank fresh from repaint in September 1948. This was one of only five members of the class to receive malachite green livery although all had reverted to lined black by March 1953. The 'M7' design was widespread throughout the former LSWR system and operated on such wide variety of duties as carriage shunting at Clapham Junction and branch line duties in the West Country. Generally they were popular with crews brought up on them but others introduced to them tended to push the engines too hard, with consequent problems over steaming. With one exception, all the class survived into the 1950s, after which general age and branch line closures reduced the amount of work available to them. No. 30038 survived until February 1958 and was then sixty years old.

Originally part of the mainland system but later transferred to the Isle of Wight and renumbered, here is former no. W13 at Eastleigh possibly after its last trip back across the Solent, 8 May 1949. Of interest also is the small crane in the background. Rarely photographed, this obscure yet essential workhorse was used to remove the piles of clinker and ashes associated with the coaling stage nearby; without this the depot would have quickly ground to a standstill. (129)

Considered to be the ugliest engine design in the country, the Bulleid 'Q1' class was basically austere yet entirely functional. Introduced in 1942 at a time of necessary austerity, the class fulfilled a useful need hauling heavy freight traffic, yet also possessed a remarkable turn of speed when called upon to work the occasional passenger train. They did however have two particular weaknesses: limited brake power was available and in consequence many an anxious moment would have been passed on the footplate when in charge of a typical unfitted freight; also, when running tender first movement could be best described as 'lively', although there is no record of any incidents that resulted. Seen here is a brace of the type, no. C21 still carrying its original Southern identification, while no. 33024 has been renumbered.

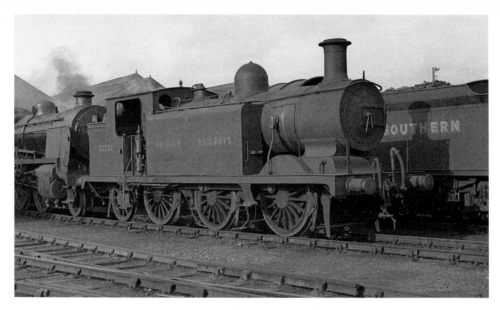

Carrying the number 32553, this former LBSCR 0–6–2T poses outside Eastleigh on an unreported date. Of particular note is the air pump attached to the cab side, a feature of a number of former Brighton design engines. These pumps had a habit of sticking from time to time, and it was not uncommon to see the fireman persuading it to work again with the aid of a coal pick or other similar implement.

Impressive from the side, this is the doyenne of the 'Lord Nelson' class, no. 30850 in early BR livery outside Eastleigh shed, probably *c.* 1948. Originally intended for express work, the introduction of the numerous Bulleid 'Pacifics' meant that the class was relegated to other duties, although certain crews preferred their predictable behaviour and to the fitters they were a straightforward machine. During the 1950s the class was employed primarily on main line secondary passenger work, together with boat-train services from Waterloo to Southampton.

Another former LBSCR design at Eastleigh was this 'E1' tank no. s2133, which had once been named 'Picardy'. Records show that two of the class were allocated to Eastleigh in April 1950, the one pictured and also no. 32147, duties being general shunting together with work at Southampton Docks. They were not universally popular away from their home territory, however, principally on account of their cramped footplate conditions, poor acceleration and sharp braking. In the form shown no. s2133 survived until November 1952; although allocated number 32133 this was never carried.

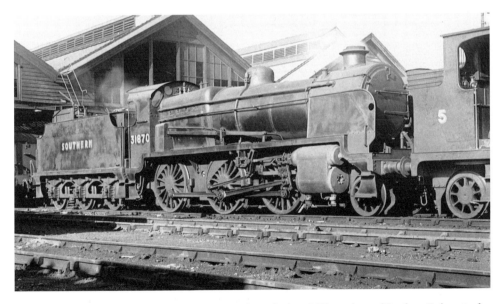

A rather travel-stained 'N' class 2–6–0 no. 31870 outside Eastleigh with BR number and Southern Railway tender. Rarely seen in detail but clear from the photograph is the original wooden front of the running shed, which was rebuilt in the 1950s. In view of the use the shed had over the years it is perhaps surprising that this timber survived, although as can be seen a number of the original glass panels intended to admit light to the inside are no more.

So successful were the original Urie design 'S15' class on heavy goods work that the design was perpetuated by his successor R.E.L. Maunsell; another fifteen engines of similar design were built between 1927 and 1936. A number of differences existed between the two types, most noticeable of which were the straight running plate and different cab. Although intended for freight work those stationed at Exmouth Junction were also used on passenger trains to Salisbury, while until electrification they also found work on passenger trains between Waterloo and Portsmouth, which they handled with ease. Seen here at Eastleigh in May 1949, no. 30838 (as it became) was one of the final batch to be withdrawn, in September 1965. (131)

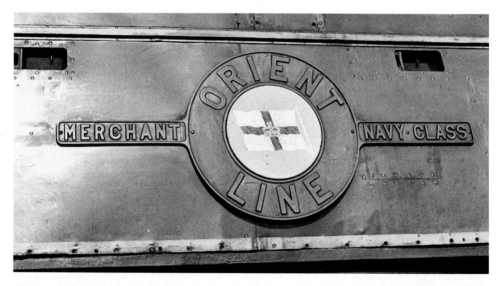

This was the right-hand side name-plate to 35008 'Orient Line', identified as such because the ship's flag flew towards the rear on each side of the engine. The engine itself is clearly in original condition, although it was later rebuilt minus air-smooth casing. Particular features of note are the rib joining the panels and running along above the top of the name-plate, and the two open slides which afforded access to the sand fillers. Unfortunately these were not always closed, thus allowing the ingress of water and dirt, and preventing accurate use of sanding facilities. (132)

Left: Beautifully clean, this plate was attached to no. 21C160, later 34060, which was seen at Eastleigh on 14 May 1949. At this time the malachite green livery was still worn, although this would be changed later. This engine was subsequently rebuilt in November 1960 and survived until the very end of steam in July 1967. At that time one of the name-plates was presented to the RAF and the other sold to a private buyer. (157)

Below: Another member of the same class, no. 21C154, later 34054, and probably at about the same time. When clean the steam engine could be an attractive piece of machinery, but by its very design attracted dirt and grime. Sadly railway pay in the 1950s was in direct competition with industry where the same wages could be earned without the dirt and unsocial hours. The result was a spiral of decline which partly contributed to the end of steam itself.

Posed outside the office block at Eastleigh on 14 May 1949, former PDSWJR 0–6–2T no. 30757 'Earl of Mount Edgcumbe' appears fresh from its repaint and almost ready to return to its regular duties around Plymouth and Callington. Of particular interest in the view is the massive office block, much of which was originally built as a dormitory for visiting locomotive crews, although whether much sleep would have been possible in the environment is perhaps doubtful. Surmounting the building was a large water tank, water being drawn direct from the River Itchen; when it was occasionally cleaned out it would afford a generous bounty of fish. (158/159)

Fresh from overhaul and without any evidence of ownership detail, 'M7' tank no. 30051 poses alongside 34051 'Winston Churchill' on 14 May 1949. Between the engines it is just possible to glimpse the nearly full cycle rack, most men either walking or cycling to work – as few apart from the foreman, perhaps, would have the luxury of a car. (160)

Probably taken just before the previous photograph, no. 34051 is seen again here but this time in slightly grimy condition. Many of these photographs and of other sheds show a line of locomotives end to end, which was the recognised way of stabling. It was up to the foreman to ensure that each machine was in the correct place for the next tour of duty, and accordingly at least one shunting engine and crew would be engaged perhaps full time in positioning and moving engines ready for repair, preparation or duty.

Fresh from overhaul and repaint, no. 34051 'Winston Churchill' presents a clean appearance, although in stark contrast to M7 30124 just discernible behind, 14 May 1949. 34051 would achieve distinction in 1965 by hauling its namesake's funeral train, and was subsequently saved for preservation although not currently in working condition. (161)

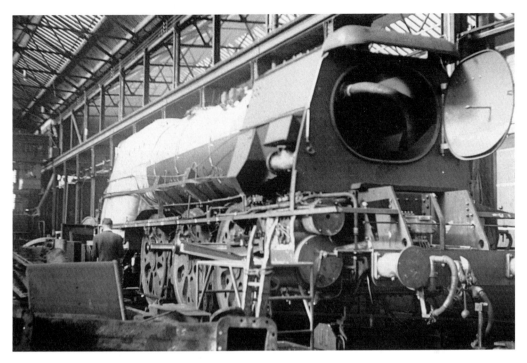

Two views inside the neighbouring works, unfortunately undated and unidentified. They show one of the Bulleid 'Pacific' breed in a state of undress, streamlined casing unattached, although aside from this and the lack of front bogie and rear pony truck the engine is basically complete. While this may well be an engine in for overhaul it is perhaps more likely that the views depict the construction of one of a batch of 'Pacifics' at Eastleigh.

Looking clean and spruce, 'L12' class 4–4–0 reposes in the May sunshine outside the front of Eastleigh shed, 1949. Allocated to Guildford from 1946 undoubtedly this was its last repaint, for despite appearing in reasonable external condition it was to survive only until June 1951. (162)

Complete with lamp standard apparently growing out of the chimney, Maunsell variant 'King Arthur' class 4–6–0 no. 30784 'Sir Nerovens' awaits its next turn of duty outside Eastleigh shed on 14 May 1949. At the time this was one of six members of the class allocated to Eastleigh, which found regular employment on main line services including the through workings via Basingstoke to Reading and Oxford. (164)

Large tank engines were not a prominent feature of the former LSWR system, with two notable exceptions. One of these was the five members of the H16 class: although originally intended for shunting and pilot goods working around the London yards consideration was also given to their use on Bournemouth line semi-fast services. Accordingly in 1922 trials were carried out with ten coaches on these workings, but rough riding when working bunker first allied to restricted water capacity relegated them once more to their original duties. No. 518, later 30518, is seen here at Eastleigh on an unrecorded date. The class was later a feature of the area in its final years from 1960 to 1962 when the engines provided power for the heavy Fawley oil trains between the terminal and the Eastleigh yards. (170)

LBSCR 'B4' 4–4–0 at Eastleigh on an unreported date – not to be confused with the little LSWR 0–4–0 dock tanks of the same class designation. This must have been one of Wally's earlier photographs for records show no. 2066 was withdrawn as early as May 1935. Originally used on the fastest trains on the former Brighton line they were quickly displaced, and many members of the class afforded good service until final demise in 1951. (171)

An 'M7' tank in everyday condition. No. 30479 was one of the last batch of engines built in 1911 and was also one of the last survivors in May 1964. (178)

A brief interlude at Southampton Central, where Wally recorded 21C153 'Sir Keith Park' on what was a coastal service from Brighton in about 1948. Despite the intensity of services around Southampton there was no separate locomotive shed for the station, engines being provided from Eastleigh less than 6 miles north.

Affording station pilot duties at about the same time is 'M7' class 0–4–4T no. 48. This engine and its crew would be responsible for the attachment and detaching of vehicles to and from trains, at a time when it was by no means uncommon for extra coaches to be provided should passenger numbers warrant such a move. Notice in the background the big signal-box controlling the area; it still survives as office accommodation today.

This time it is the turn of 'U' class 2–6–0 no. 31622 to be pilot at Southampton, although for the present it simmers in the bay known as Platform 5. This engine had commenced life as a tank engine named 'River Meon', although to some naming engines after waterways was considered unlucky. Following the disastrous Sevenoaks accident in 1927 all were rebuilt in the form seen here, with names removed.

A delightfully sunny 18 May 1949 sees 'N' class no. 1807 awaiting the road west from Platform 3. The sylvan setting is heightened by the trees on the far side of the station, although it must be said that the station was reasonably central, located for ease of access to both the town and the new, western docks. (144)

For many years it was the practice for Eastleigh to provide a standby engine at Southampton Central during the mornings in case of any failure or difficulty on a down working. The engine later worked a stopping service to Bournemouth should it not have been required. Such a provision may now appear to be a luxury but it was by no means unusual at various sites around the country during the age of steam, and did not imply failures were necessarily commonplace. Performing the task on 9 May 1950 was 30855 'Robert Blake', apparently still in light green livery. (693)

A view now of some of the services around Southampton Central, commencing with no. 35029, later 'Ellerman Lines', although at the time of the photograph (11 May 1949) the name-plate was fitted yet covered up awaiting an official naming ceremony. The train is a Waterloo to Bournemouth and possibly Weymouth working, with a motley collection of stock – again not untypical for the period. (205)

From a similar vantage point and on the same day 'S15' 4–6–0 no. 30499 affords unusual motive power for what may well be an excursion working from the LNER – judging by the coaching stock. Credence then is given to the use of these engines on such workings and which was probably destined for one of the coastal resorts. (206)

Wally moved his position a few yards further westwards to capture 34040 'Crewkerne' with an unusual West of England headcode leaving Southampton on 1 October 1949. Was this a diverted service routed via Romsey? Notice the engine retains its original shape cab, while the first vehicle is typically Southern in the form of the bogie utility van, some of which could still be seen in departmental service nearly forty years later. (486)

With its intended destination probably somewhere on the coast, 'U' class 2–6–0 no. 31626, once named 'River Sid', leaves Southampton westwards, 9 July 1949. Clearly it was a warm day when the photograph was taken, as there is no obvious steam to be seen from the departing engine. It would be exactly eighteen years later to the day that steam would cease working on the Southern, although no. 31626 had been retired earlier in January 1964. (313)

Having referred to their use on excursion and other types of special service it is pleasing to be able to illustrate the point. Here 'D15' no. 30469 is seen leaving Southampton westbound with what is clearly an excursion working, made up of a variety of stock originating from both the GWR and LMR. One passenger at least in the first coach is intent on leaning some distance from the window. The view was taken in the height of summer, 14 August 1949. The engine was withdrawn from service in December 1951. (377)

Turning the camera around Wally captured another 'U boat', as they were sometimes referred to, this time no. 31618, formerly 'River Hamble', about to enter the station on a train of Great Western stock, 14 May 1949. This was probably a working from Salisbury, the eventual destination of which would be Portsmouth via Netley and Fareham. (141)

A real gem this time, with a Drummond design '700' class 0–6–0, no. 30350, at the head of a local train of compartment stock. The date is October 1949, and such services with similar locomotives and stock continued to operate until well into the 1950s, superseded only with the advent of the 'Hampshire' diesel/electric units. (485)

A final view of Southampton, with the return working of an ex-LNER set behind no. 30740 'Merlin' on 14 May 1949 – as can be seen reconverted to burn coal. At least eight coaches can be counted although there were probably more; a good head of steam will be required for the run north of Eastleigh towards Winchester and Basingstoke. (142)

Returning now towards Eastleigh, and a location not favoured by many photographers: Mount Pleasant level-crossing just south of St Denys, where a road crossing went over the four running lines. Fortunately there was a footbridge for the benefit of pedestrians, as with the almost continual procession of trains at weekends the gates would remain across the road for long periods. For the record the engine is no. 34105 'Swanage' and the date is 8 July 1950. (897)

Back at Eastleigh, and no. 35015 'Rotterdam Lloyd' is depicted in freshly repainted condition on 12 June 1949, still with the original cover over the slidebars. Despite having received a wedge-shape cab front the tender would appear to be unaltered; the tenders like the engines were subject to considerable modification and rebuilding over the years. (209)

Exemplifying its massive proportions is no. 30488 of the 'H15' class, ready to leave Eastleigh on 27 March 1949 ready for its tour of duty. Before leaving the crew would have booked on duty perhaps one hour early to prepare and check the engine, an accepted part of the work. (150)

The first of the 'Leader' class is towed into the works at Eastleigh for weighing and inspection, having previously arrived from Brighton, 26 June 1949. The whole 'Leader' project was then in its infancy and the trials and tribulations of successive failures had yet to materialise. (See my books on the subject published by Sutton Publishing for further details.) (255/6)

On the same day that 'Leader' was arriving at the works, Wally also recorded a reasonably clean 'E4' tank no. 32557 in the shed yard. From the look of the paintwork there is some evidence of recent priming from the chimney, and the streaks running down the side indicate that recently the engine had slipped and carried an amount of water over into the cylinders. (261)

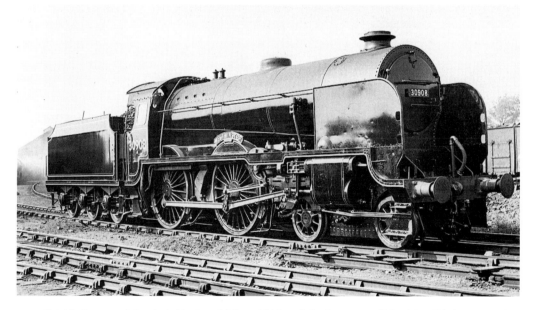

Outside the rear of the shed this time, 26 June 1949, and the first time a 'Schools' or 'V' class engine has appeared within these pages. This example of what can only be described as surely the best 4–4–0 to run in this country is no. 30908 'Westminster', newly turned out in lined black and very smart as a result. For their size the 'Schools' class engines were capable of prodigious load haulage and were employed throughout the Southern system until displaced by electrification in 1961/2. (262)

A not so well-kempt member of the class, no. 30932 'Blundells', minus one smoke deflector, rods and half the cab roof – so no doubt awaiting works attention. The cause of the contretemps is unfortunately not recorded. It was not unusual for locomotives to be stored in the vicinity of the shed until there was room available within the works, where accommodation could be decidedly limited at times.

A final view of a 'Schools' class, a rather travel-stained no. 907 'Dulwich' on 10 April 1948. The engine is fitted with a large diameter chimney and multiple jet blastpipe as advocated by Bulleid, although there was only a limited increase in performance as these were already good engines. They were also reasonably light on repairs, averaging some 1,000 miles in service weekly and needing works overhaul only every two years or so. As no. 30907 the engine was retired in September 1961 having run over a million miles in thirty years. (33)

Now to a design dating back to 1880. This is an Adams '0395' class 0–6–0 as BR no. 30578 in beautiful external condition at Eastleigh, 9 July 1949. The surviving members of the class based at the depot were employed primarily on works shunting and also local freight work to locations such as Otterbourne Siding and Winchester Chesil. During the winter months it was also not uncommon for one to be fitted semi-permanently with a snow plough, although fortunately this was rarely used. (314)

Fresh from overhaul, 30788 'Sir Urie of the Mount' awaits its first duties at Eastleigh. The engine has received a repaint in what were still standard Southern colours, including the green top half to the smoke deflectors. At this stage no definite ruling on future liveries had been received from the headquarters of the Railway Executive at Marylebone Road, although when it was a number of engines including no. 30788 would be subjected to a further repaint.

Another 'King Arthur', this time no. 30801 'Sir Meliot de Logres', sporting a different livery in that the smoke deflectors are plain black, 9 July 1949. To many this style was to be preferred to that seen in the previous photograph, although it was also the subject of much argument among youthful spotters at the end of the station platform! Some of the names used (all were characters in the legends of 'King Arthur') were obscure and not always recognised by the public. (320)

A Brighton 'Terrier' tank in plain black at Eastleigh, 14 August 1949. These diminutive engines dated back to the 1870s and yet were retained for working places like the Hayling Island line from Havant, upon which they were the only engines allowed. Several have been preserved and it is still possible to travel behind one, albeit dwarfed by the following coach, on both the Bluebell and Kent & East Sussex railways. (378)

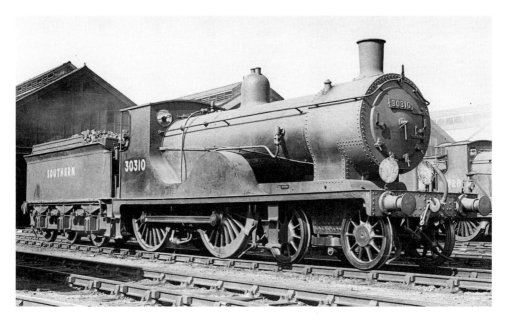

More typical of the engines to be seen in so far as condition was concerned is this view of 'T9' class 4–4–0 no. 30310 outside the shed on 21 August 1949. Cleaners were often in short supply at Eastleigh, the boys who commenced in the grade rapidly put on to firing duties to cover shortages on the footplate. As such a first grounding for the aspiring engine driver could be shunting the yards at Eastleigh or even a trip on an engine such as a 'T9', where it was very much a question of 'sink or swim'. (387)

Cowes, Isle of Wight, where a supermarket now stands on the site of the station. Until 1966, though, trains would leave the curved platforms for Newport and the rest of the system, this view of W35 in 1949 typical and unchanging until the demise of steam on the line to Newport. (404)

Interlude at Salisbury, and at the east end of the station no. 30773 'Sir Lavaine' makes what appears to be a cautious start on a wet rail with a Waterloo-bound service, 26 August 1949. To the right of the engine is the former Great Western station, the two routes running parallel with each other for some distance westwards until a parting of the ways occurred at Wilton. (413)

Another eastbound service departing, this time in the care of 35016 'Elders Fyffes'. Following the tragic accident at Salisbury in 1906 caused by excess speed on a curve, nearly all passenger trains were booked to call at the station, the one exception being the short-lived 'Devon Belle' Pullman – although this did stop for engine changing at Wilton. (412)

The layout of the platforms at Salisbury afforded ideal vantage points for the enthusiast, particularly the branch platform from which this view was taken, 1 July 1950. From here local services via Fordingbridge would depart, and also the stopping trains to Romsey and beyond. On the main line Urie design 'King Arthur' no. 30452 'Sir Meliagrance' is seen making a spirited getaway with a train of Bulleid stock and complete with useful train reporting number. Ahead of the engine is the spacious milk loading platform, from which almost complete train loads would be dispatched to the London creameries. (865)

Venturing now to the western end of the station, and one of the first series 'S15' class 4–6–0s, no. 30475, is seen appropriately at home on a freight. Alongside also is a delightful LSWR lattice post signal, while in the background a number of vans are stored in the area of what was the former Great Western station. (615)

No. 34051 'Winston Churchill' again, depicted at Salisbury on 21 August 1949 just three months after the repaint at Eastleigh pictured earlier. Clearly in that time some miles have been covered for the pristine shine has vanished to be replaced by a dull finish, and evidence of being wiped by successive oily rags. (414)

On what may well be a diverted Paddington service, 70026 'Polar Star' awaits departure at the head of a train of former Great Western stock, 4 August 1953. Members of the 'Britannia' class were no strangers to the area, with three having been allocated to the Southern for a time, while others were borrowed in May 1953 to cover a temporary storage of power following an incident with a broken axle on a member of the 'Merchant Navy' class. This led to the whole class being withdrawn for examination. (1177)

A more usual sight at Salisbury, with no. 34037 'Clovelly' at the head of a Portsmouth to Bristol train in February 1952. At this time 'Clovelly' was less than six years old and would survive in the form seen until March 1958 when a total rebuild, involving removal of the air smooth casing, took place together with a number of major mechanical modifications. In its new form the engine was a regular performer on the Western Section of the Southern and survived until the very end of steam on 9 July 1967. (616)

Westwards from the platform and the expansive track layout is apparent, the Great Western lines on the right. Entering the station is 'M7' no. 30041 on a three coach local, although it is not clear if the train will terminate or continue perhaps towards Andover. On the left can be seen the top of one of the Salisbury signal-boxes. The mechanical signals and points on the former South Western side were controlled by a low pressure pneumatic system, which gave years of reliable service. (614)

The Great Western also had a station at Salisbury, which was the destination of their line from Westbury via Warminster. Much freight traffic used the route, one example being here behind 'Mogul' no. 7302 passing the former GWR signal-box on 8 May 1954. (1296)

During the 1950s the roof of the engine shed was totally rebuilt; this 1954 view of 'U' class 2–6–0 no. 31636 shows the work taking place. Salisbury shed survived until the end of steam, after which it became a collecting point for redundant engines before final dispatch to the South Wales scrap yards. (1344)

A final view in the Salisbury area, with no. 35022 'Holland America Line' shortly to enter the station with a train from Exeter, 18 February 1950. To the right and at a slightly higher level can be seen the former Great Western route, although this is now abandoned, a new junction at Wilton meaning all traffic is concentrated on the former LSWR lines. (611)

Returning to Eastleigh on 4 September 1949, and a beautifully clean example of the 'Merchant Navy' class, no. 35009 'Shaw Savill', in marked contrast to the engines either side. At this time the first style of BR crest, cruelly referred to as the cycling lion, has been added – although it will be seen the engine still retains its original cab and tender design. (441)

By comparison this is 'West Country' class 4–6–2, no. 34003 'Plymouth' on shed the same day. The 'West Country' class and their identical counterparts the 'Battle of Britain' design were outwardly similar to the 'Merchant Navy' design, although they were slightly smaller and lighter and thus able to possess a wide route availability. (442)

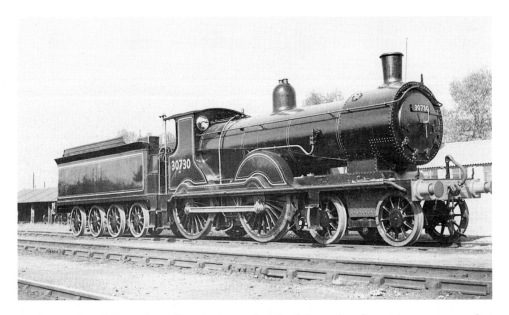

Another view from the same day, with Eastleigh paint shop clearly having been busy – as witness immaculate 'T9' no. 30730 complete with what was referred to as its watercart tender. Designed by Duguld Drummond, these engines were fitted with a steam reverser, meaning little effort was required by the driver when altering the point of cut-off for steam entering the cylinders. Just visible also is the large handbrake on the tender, which would no doubt be screwed on hard at the time the view was taken. (444)

Away from clean engines and to 'D15' class 4–4–0 no. s465 at Eastleigh in September 1949. Although not yet with full BR number, the engine would become no. 30465, and was destined to be the last survivor of the class – being finally withdrawn in January 1956 and cut up at Brighton. (480)

Another visitor of the LBSCR 'K' class depicted on-shed, 12 November 1949. The view was taken at the rear of the shed amid the usual clutter. The hard-pressed foreman rarely had sufficient men or machines available for an easy life. (525)

Attractive in lined black livery is no. 30931 'Kings Wimbledon', with the well-known coal stack just visible in front of the engine, 12 November 1949. This latter item was a long wall of coal several feet high and equally thick, laid down by hand as insurance in the event of interrupted supplies. To prevent the coal 'going off' as would otherwise occur, sections were used and replaced at intervals, the whole issue a highly labour-intensive activity – yet typical of big steam sheds country-wide. (527)

Two views now of the big 'Z' class 0–8–0T design, introduced by Maunsell between March and September 1929 from Brighton Works, costing £6,145 apiece. Intended for heavy yard shunting they eventually travelled far afield, and were also employed on banking trains up the severe gradient between the two stations at Exeter. All eight members of the class were withdrawn in the massive cull of steam in 1962. (528)

No. 30956 of the class at Eastleigh on an unreported date. Between December 1942 and December 1943 this was one of three examples of the type transferred to War Department duties at Stranraer in Scotland, where it carried a grey livery with yellow lettering, crimson coupling rods and white buffer beams. An electric light was also affixed front and rear. The more usual black was reinstated upon return to Southern metals. For many years one of the class was also the regular shunter at Eastleigh East yard until ousted by BR or ex-LMS tank engines.

The former LBSCR had at one time advocated the use of large tank engines for the majority of its passenger services, and the twenty-seven members of the 'I3' class were so utilised from the time of their introduction in late 1907 onwards, until superseded by still larger designs. The story of their final years is by no means untypical in that expensive repairs, principally to frames and firebox, were not considered worthwhile and when these became essential withdrawal resulted. An additional problem existed with several of the engines in that the side tanks were known to leak and no amount of welding could stem the flow. This in turn led to the need for frequent water stops and limited route availability. No. 32026 survived until August 1951, with the last of the class going in May 1953. This photograph dates from 12 November 1949. (535/6)

Formerly in use on the Horsham line until that was electrified, the 'I1x' class was another medium size LBSCR tank design. With only a four coupled wheel arrangement a considerable amount of available weight was not used for adhesion, with the result that they were never the equal of the later 2–6–2T and 2–6–4T designs. No. 2002 is seen in obvious store at what may well be Bognor on an unreported date; it is unlikely that it ever ran again.

At least six members of the same class await their fate at Eastleigh probably in about 1948, depicted outside the front of the shed. From the line-up only one engine can be positively identified, no. 2006, although the second one may be no. 2004.

On territory not far from Wally's home now, and no. 30471 nears Swanwick, 26 February 1950. This was perhaps a typical local service of the period, consisting of three coaches of LSWR design and a steam engine previously pensioned off from more exacting duties. (622)

On 26 April the previous year 'M7' class 0–4–4T no. 30674 was on a similar working, with one member of the footplate crew keen to get in the photograph – was it by prior arrangement? The 'Southern' lettering has still to be replaced; the engine is otherwise in black livery, with the coaching stock probably dark green. (76)

More exacting work this time for 'D15' no. 466 leaving Fareham on 26 February 1950. The load is one of six bogies and a van, four of the coaches at least to former GWR design, indicating that this is probably a Salisbury or Bristol working. (621)

The other side of Southampton now to Nursling, were on 9 May 1950 no. 30855 'Robert Blake' has charge of a Bournemouth line working. The first three vehicles are coupled together as set no. 978. For many years the Southern Railway and its successor the Southern Region of BR formed vehicles into three, six or eight coach sets, one advantage being that regular passengers could become familiar with train layouts. This particular service, though, would appear to contain a motley collection of vehicles, the actual number not possible to determine. (695)

No. 34036 seen running un-named, but later 'Westward Ho', near to Nursling with an eight coach service from Salisbury. Today much of the area around the railway at this point is covered with industrial estates, although at the time it was open land. (696)

One final view of a train at Nursling, with 'N' class 2–6–0 no. 1792 (again coupled to Great Western stock) working hard past Wally's camera. The destination was probably Bristol, with an engine change taking place at Salisbury. (697)

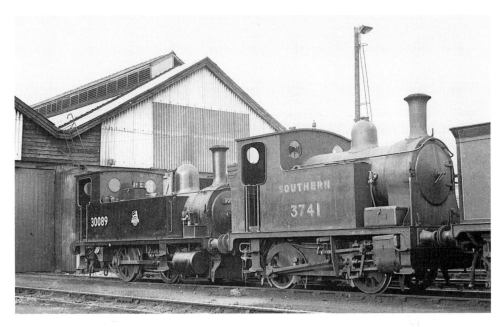

Returning once again to Eastleigh on 4 March 1950, and two diminutive tank engines in the shape of nos 30089 and 3741. No. 30089 was a member of the 'B4' class, principally intended for dock shunting but which also found employment at locations such as Winchester and Guildford. No. 3741 was a member of the 'C14' class, originally intended for work on single coach motor trains. The two surviving members of the class, dating back to 1906, were employed shunting the Town Quay at Southampton and also Redbridge Sleeper Works until the late 1950s. (630)

A rather grimy 'B4' carrying the name 'Dinan', but in reality no. 746. This was one of a number of engines of the class introduced by Adams from 1891 onwards, intended for dock and station shunting. They were a success from the outset, with the majority later working at Southampton Docks where most were also named. Three survived until late 1963, by which time their work had been taken over by either the USA tanks or more modern diesel machines. Happily two are preserved, although not this particular engine which was an early casualty in November 1948.

Within the works yard now and bordered by the carriage sidings alongside the Portsmouth line, 'L11' class 4-4-0 no. 30442 is seen fresh from overhaul in about March 1950 and probably awaiting its first running-in turn. This was the engine's last works visit as it was withdrawn on 22 November 1951, with probably its last duty being a freight on the line from Andover that same afternoon. Clearly the works possessed some spare capacity at that time for it was cut up at the rear of Eastleigh Works the very next day.

Also resplendent fresh from overhaul is 'M7' No. 30133 with the small BR emblem favoured at that time, 25 March 1950. Livery is black lined out with red and white, not unlike the former LNWR style, which when clean suited these engines well. (647)

As BR no. 30589, 'C14' reposes in the March sunshine at Eastleigh, 1950. Seen here fitted with 'B4' style chimney, the engine was used on a special over the branch to Bishops Waltham in June 1952, when it was reported as having reached nearly 35 m.p.h. – a considerable feat for an engine with wheels only 3 ft in diameter. It survived until June 1957. (649)

Another of Wally's 1930s photographs, this time an Adams design 'X2', depicted as Southern no. 587 at Eastleigh. A typical late Victorian express design, the classic lines were similar to those seen on several railways of the time and indicative of the fashion of the period. Relegated to secondary duties as early as 1903/4, the class continued to perform well on both West of England and Bournemouth line duties until the early 1930s, when scrapping commenced. No. 587 survived until August 1937.

Recorded on the scrap line at Eastleigh in August 1949, this is no. 657, a survivor of the film *Oh Mr. Porter* which had last run in service as far back as September 1940. The engine did have one further period of use in 1941, when stripped of pistons and valve rods it was towed to Exmouth Junction for use supplying steam to the newly introduced 'Merchant Navy' class engines so that these might be kept in steam continually. It performed such tasks until March 1941 when it was towed back to Eastleigh to repose, as seen. The end would not be long coming, for in November 1949 it was broken up at Horley. (391)

A clean example of the 'Q1' class no. 33022, 16 April 1950. Records show Wally took just four photographs on that day, all around the shed area; the others showed nos 30506, 30721 and 30700. (664)

Newly outshopped is former WD 2–10–0 no. 90763, 22 April 1950. At this stage the engine still retains its Westinghouse air pump although this was removed later on. Never as numerous as the 2–8–0 version of the 'Austerity' design depicted earlier in this book, a number of the 2–10–0 type were retained by the Army for some years as well as some which continued at work in Greece and Turkey. At least two of the batch survive in preservation today although others may still be dumped, 'somewhere near the Mediterranean'. (666)

The turntable at Eastleigh was alongside the front of the shed; part of the works complex is visible on the left. In this superb study of 'U' class no. 31794 on 25 March 1950 both members of the crew can be seen, with the engine in clean lined black livery. (659/60)

Ex-works on 23 April 1950 is 'Lord Nelson' no. 30856 'Lord St Vincent', within the shed complex. By the look of things it would appear both it and neighbouring no. 32103 have emerged from overhaul and been towed

into the shed. No. 30856 at least displays some evidence of priming from the chimney, which otherwise mars a spotless machine. (669/70)

Seen outside this time: another view of no. 30856. Did Wally ask for the engine to be moved for a photograph? In the background are the water tower, office block and water softener. Hard chalk water in the Hampshire area meant it was necessary for treatment to be provided to prevent the accumulation of scale and deposits within the boiler, which would otherwise impair steaming and increase boiler wear. (671)

North of Eastleigh now and no. 30457 'Sir Bedivere' is near Basingstoke on 27 June 1954. The train is made up of Bulleid design coaching stock, partly in green and partly the crimson and cream livery of the period. (1328)

On 23 April 1950 Wally visited Reading and recorded views at both the former GWR station as well as the Southern shed. The latter was the home of several former SECR designs including 'D' class 4–4–0 no. 1740, which dated back to February 1902. (659)

The same engine seen against a backdrop of the big GWR Reading East signal-box, with essential telegraph pole nearby. At this stage no. 1740 had less than twelve months to survive and was withdrawn in March 1951 having covered in the order of 1.4 million miles. (743)

Returning to the Southampton area again, and no. 35017 'Belgian Marine' is in charge of the down 'Bournemouth Belle' on Redbridge Causeway, 9 May 1950. The bridge in the background carries the railway over the River Test, which was one of two fresh water feeders into Southampton Water. (694)

A few miles down the Fareham line from Eastleigh is the station at Botley, once the junction for the branch to Bishops Waltham. It was also within the growing area for soft fruit and for many years trainloads of strawberries would be dispatched during the season to the London markets. On more mundane duties, no. 30749 'Sir Torre' is leaving the station in the direction of Eastleigh on 9 May 1950, in charge of a four coach stopping service. (698)

A tongue-in-cheek inclusion, but taken by Wally, is this view of no. 4943 'Marrington Hall' near Cosham with what appears to be a three coach LSWR set, 13 May 1950. Former GWR engines were not unknown visitors to the area but would usually work back on their own trains. This may well have been the return of the engine following a special working, although rather than running light it is made to perform a revenue earning duty. (702)

Returning to Eastleigh again on 14 May 1950, and no. 82 of the LSWR 'B4' class is seen ahead of an unidentified 'King Arthur'. This engine would be renumbered 30082 under British Railways, and was probably gainfully employed at either Winchester, Bournemouth or within the Southampton Docks complex. (708)

A newly outshopped member of the same class, no. 30094, seen at Eastleigh before a return to its more usual haunts around Plymouth. At the latter location the 'B4's were engaged on Turnchapel and Stonehouse Pool workings until displaced by diesels in early 1957. Both it and sister engine no. 30089 left Plymouth for the last time on 14 February that year and probably returned to Eastleigh from where no. 30094 was withdrawn the following month, although sister engine 30089 had a further five years of life ahead. (730)

Assorted front ends at Eastleigh in May 1950, the nearest being 'L12' no. 433. The presence of other stabled locomotives prevented a full view of the comparative types, which even so display the individual styles of at least three separate designers. (755)

Beautifully clean no. 34005 'Barnstaple' ex-works, 28 May 1950. This was one of the early 'West Country' class engines and had been introduced from Brighton in July 1945. The engine is also carrying long smoke deflectors, a feature of all of the class used on the interchange trials of 1948. Previously the livery carried was a malachite green, although the dark green displayed here seemed to suit the type better. (756)

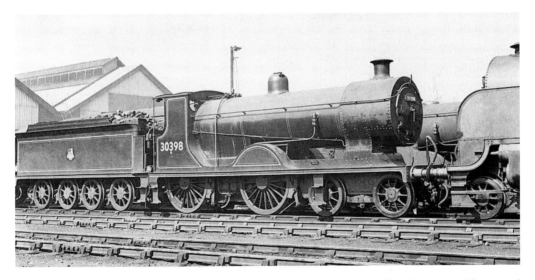

'S11' class 4–4–0 no. 30398 photographed in BR ownership, May 1950. Although in reasonable external condition it was reported that the mechanical condition of many of the class was by this time poor, and they spent much of their time laid aside pending withdrawal. In the background the front of the shed has been replaced with corrugated sheeting, a distinctly unfavourable comparison to the condition displayed in some of the earlier views. (759)

Basingstoke shed this time, and a somewhat grimy 'S15' of the first Urie design awaiting what is probably a Salisbury line working on 3 June 1950. Basingstoke was obviously short of cleaners at that time as only the cabside number has received a wipe over, the rest of the engine being a dirty grey. (135)

Also on-shed on the same day was a former LBSCR 'Baltic' tank now rebuilt as 4–6–0 no. 32329 'Stephenson'. There were seven members of the class, all of which were loaned to the GWR for a period during the 1940s, with this particular engine going to the GWR shed at Exeter. It must be said that not all were in tip top condition at that time and the GWR were probably glad to get rid of them later on. Following the return to peace the class was based at Basingstoke, working secondary duties to Waterloo, Reading, Portsmouth and Salisbury until displaced by more modern steam power. At the time the photograph was taken, no. 2329 had been in lined black livery for just two months, and was destined to receive two further repaints before being taken out of service in July 1956. (796)

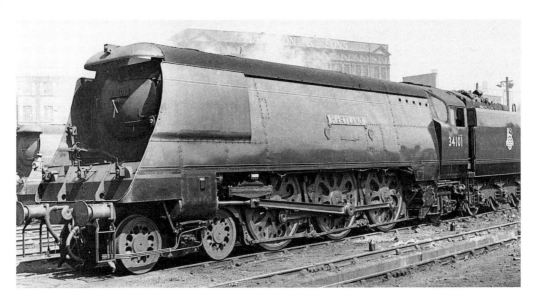

A week later, on 10 June 1950, Wally's records report him visiting Stewarts Lane, where no. 34101 'Hartland' is seen outside the shed. This shed was the home of the redoubtable R. 'Dick' Hardy, shedmaster for a period during the 1950s, whose exploits at attempting to secure sufficient locomotives and men are well known. No. 34101 was one of several of the type then allocated to 'The Lane' and would be utilised on the Kent line services, including boat-trains from Victoria. (801)

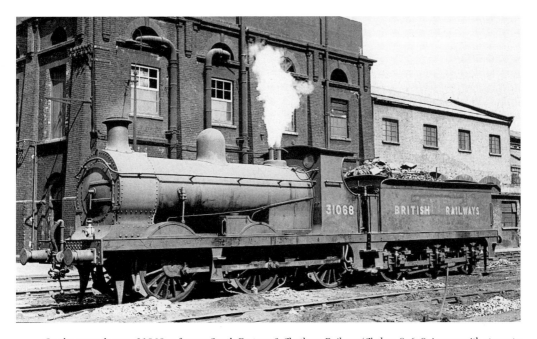

On the same day no. 31068, a former South Eastern & Chatham Railway 'C' class 0–6–0, is seen with steam to spare at the Bricklayers Arms depot. Used in the London area for local freight work as well as transfer duties between yards, they were a common sight throughout the former Eastern Section for many years. No. 31068 survived until October 1961, at which time it had covered well over a million miles since being built in 1903. (817)

Also at 'The Brick', as it was known, was 'C2X' no. 32525, which would be employed on similar workings. This was a former LBSCR engine, and although both were intended for similar work and indeed date from a similar time, the respective designer's preferences are apparent. No. 32525 had been rebuilt from the similar 'C2' class in 1910 and remained in service until January 1962. (816)

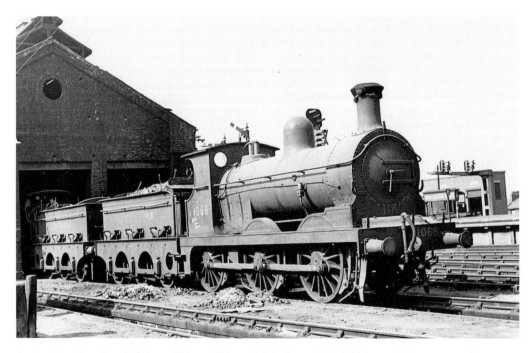

A visit to New Cross Gate shed also on 10 June 1950 revealed this former SECR 'O1' class 0–6–0 in store, complete with sacking over the chimney. Similar to, but predating the 'C' class, the earlier small tender with outside springs is visible while another member of the class, probably also stored, reposes within the shed. (823)

To Hither Green this time, and again on the same date: 30805 'Sir Constantine' has its cylinder cocks open as it moves slowly back. Originally several of the class were allocated to the depot, again for service in Kent, but the influx of large numbers of 'Pacifics' meant that by the late 1950s it was almost a rarity to see a member of the class at the depot. No. 30805 worked for forty-two years in service and was withdrawn in November 1959. (828)

Seen this time in BR livery as no. 90562, this is a former 'Austerity' 2–8–0 at Hither Green in June 1950. Referred to by some crews as members of the 'bovine' fraternity (except that they did not give milk), the class were rugged and powerful – although generally not liked by men unused to regular work on them. (829)

A final visit by Wally on 10 June was to Norwood Junction, where no. 32466 is captured in a line-up of engines. Built as no. 466 'Honour Oak' in April 1898, the engine was rebuilt in the form seen in February 1909 and survived until December 1958. (830)

Returning to Eastleigh again on 25 June 1950: Shell Mex no. 5 is seen, arrived no doubt for overhaul. The Shell company had a refinery at Hamble, with rail access from the Netley line near Hamble Halt. No. 5 worked at the location for some time, even if the idea of a steam engine within an oil refinery complex does sound strange. The refinery still exists today, although no traffic now passes by rail. (851)

Within the shed, and 35016 'Elders Fyffes' fresh from a repaint. Between the rails it is possible to notice the water hydrants, essential when boiler washing was carried out although easy to fall over at night when only limited illumination was available. (852)

Seen as no. DS3152, this is an Adams design 'G6' which, as the side tanks display, was intended for work at Meldon Quarry near Okehampton. There were thirty-four members of the class although several were withdrawn in about 1948/9 without receiving BR numbers. DS3152 had originally been Southern Railway no. 272, although it had been renumbered only a few days before Wally's photo. It remained at work until August 1960 and was replaced at Meldon by another member of the class, DS682, formerly no. 30238. (863)

To Southampton Docks now, and no. 30072 – which had been purchased by the Southern for £2,500 in 1946. To the left is another member of the class, both crews taking the time to enjoy a break from duty on 8 July 1950. (888)

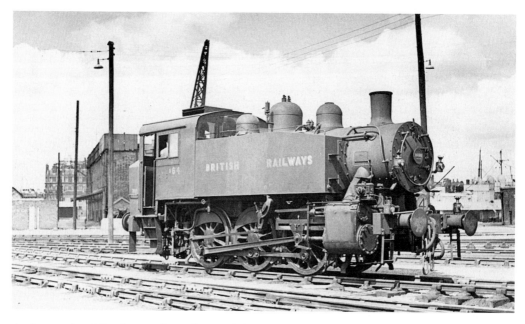

Another member of the class complete with original identification as no. 64, also within the Docks complex in 1950. Surviving until the very end of steam in July 1967, no. 30064, as it was then, spent some time at Droxford station on the Meon Valley line before being moved to the Bluebell Railway, where it saw regular service. (148)

A visit away from home for Wally on 9 July 1950, when he photographed twenty-four different engines at Ashford. Not surprisingly most, but not all, of those recorded were former SECR types, the first of a selection seen here in the shape of 'J' class 0–6–4T no. 31598. There were only five members in the class, the small number indicating perhaps that only limited success was enjoyed by the type. No. 31598 was then in its last months of existence, and was condemned in December of the same year. (898)

Another Brighton 'C2X', no. 32527, possibly in store and complete with chalked inscription on the tender – although this is not readable. For some time no. 32527 was based along with other members of the class at Three Bridges shed, and may well be seen here awaiting a works visit. It was destined to survive until November 1960. (901)

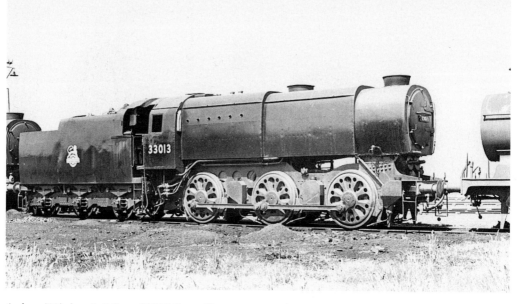

A clean 'Q1' class 0–6–0 no. 33013 (it would not remain so for long), posed next to another member of the class. To Bulleid nothing was sacred and the ugliness of the type was to some attractive. Despite their shortcomings, described earlier, the engines of this type were generally well liked. (902)

30800 'Sir Meleaus de Lile' in clean green livery. The family similarity between a number of SECR and Southern 2–6–0 and 4–6–0 types will have become apparent through the photographs, such likeness heightened by the smoke deflectors which were a feature of the various classes. (906)

Similar in outward appearance were the 'D1', 'E1' and 'L1' classes. No. 31749 was an example of the 'D1' type and originally intended for fast express work. Successful at this, they were nevertheless rapidly outpaced as trains' weights increased, although they continued to perform useful secondary service duties. Nos 31749 and 31739 were the last survivors of the class and remained in service until November 1961. (909)

Built as a three-cylinder variant of the conventional 'U' class, this is no. 31902 of class 'U1' taking on water at Ashford. Outwardly the engines of the class could be identified by the raised step at the front of the framing. The complexity of design and maintenance meant they were more expensive than the conventional two-cylinder variant. (914)

A final glimpse at Ashford on that day in the form of 'R1' tank no. 31069. This engine had a specially cut down cab and chimney for working around Canterbury, the changes doing little to enhance the otherwise pleasing lines of the design. (918)

To Eastbourne now, and former LBSCR no. 32586 'Maplehurst' seemingly dumped at the back of the shed in July 1950. A quick attempt has been made at applying new ownership details although the perhaps more hard wearing 'Southern' decal is still visible. Later, lined black would be used. Shortly after this the engine was, along with others of the class, transferred to Basingstoke for use on shunting and pilot duties, but for no. 32586 the stay was brief; it was taken out of service in 1955. (924)

Almost the opposite end of the Southern system now, with unrebuilt 'Battle of Britain' class 4–6–2 no. 34050 'Royal Observer Corps' reversing off-shed at Weymouth on 19 July 1950. Weymouth was originally a GWR station, although in consequence of regional boundary changes it passed to the control of the Southern and was destined to be the most westerly outpost of steam in July 1967. (972)

Later in the same month, Wally's camera recorded no. 30741 'Joyous Guard' leaving the station and soon to surmount the commencement of the steep climb to Bincombe Tunnel. The influence of the GWR at the location can be gauged by the fact that of the two visits made by Wally and the twenty-two photographs taken, only four were of Southern engine types. (981)

The now preserved 35018 'British India Line' seen in almost original form at Eastleigh, 19 August 1950. Notice on the rear offside driving wheel a speedometer has been added, while the engine benefits from the improved cab applied to the class from August 1947 onwards. (1031)

This time without speedometer fitment, 35011 'General Steam Navigation' resplendent in malachite green together with three yellow bands at Eastleigh, 1 October 1950. Originally built with a 280 p.s.i. boiler the pressure was reduced to 250 p.s.i. from 1952 onwards, with the intention of not only reducing maintenance costs but also in an attempt to reduce the propensity for slipping so often demonstrated by the class. (1048)

A clean 'Brighton' 'C2X' 0–6–0 no. 32528 at Eastleigh in March 1953, with an almost brand new 'Standard 4' behind. The engine is of the type fitted with underslung injectors and dual braking, while backed coal rails have been added to the tender. (1107)

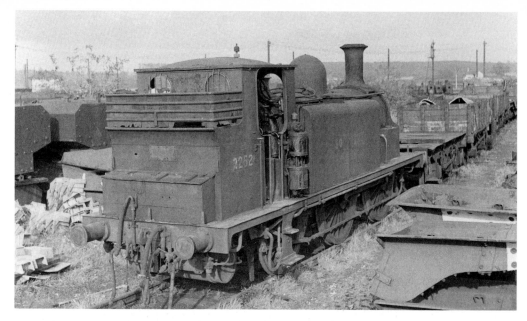

During the 1940s nine former LBSCR 'D1' class tank engines were converted to mobile fire fighting engines and equipped with suitable pumps. One of these was no. 2252, which in its new guise was based at Norwood Junction. Here, though, it is seen at the rear of the works yard at Eastleigh in October 1950 amid the various items of clutter, which in the distance also include a number of redundant boilers. Despite having been reprieved after 1945, the engine had seen only limited use after this time and was now awaiting cutting up, having been officially withdrawn during the previous month. (1055/6)

Not perhaps the best looking of the Maunsell designs, the appearance of this 'Q' class no. 30531 had been changed as early as November 1940 with the addition of large diameter chimney and was the first of the class to be so modified. In its new form it had at first been employed on an Alton goods service, and to the observer at least was a better steamer than previously – although prone to throw fire from the chimney. (1015)

The classic view of the rear of the shed, with its close proximity to the nearby airport demonstrated. Indeed one of the best views of the shed could often be gained from an aircraft! This is perhaps the scene so well remembered, with assorted lines of engines, most of which are in steam, although missing are examples of the 'Pacific' type. 6 August 1950. (1016)

Influx of the foreigners and LMS type 2–6–4T no. 42097 at Eastleigh in October 1950. Large numbers of this and the later BR 'Standard' types of tank engine meant the end for a variety of the pre-grouping types seen earlier, although the lives of the former would be cut short as a result of diesel and electric traction. (1047)

Dignity and impudence. Only thirty-nine years separate the building dates of the two engines, 3741 in 1906 and 35018 from 1945. As is inferred from their respective sizes, though, the designers' intentions were very different indeed, motor train and express passenger. (1032)

Photographs of the various Drummond design 4–6–0s are comparatively rare, and in service more so, their use almost a last resort to a struggling shed foreman. Never as successful as the 4–4–0 Drummond types, no. 30461 somehow managed to linger on in service until June 1951 and was for some time employed on milk

empties between Clapham Junction and Salisbury. The view was taken alongside the Eastleigh coaling stage during the evening of 19 August 1950, as witness the lengthening shadows. After this the engine had but ten months of service left. (1036)

Also at Eastleigh is 2–6–0 no. 76007, the first of a number of these engines which would be based at the shed. With their high running plate and exposed wheels they were intended for ease of maintenance and reliability in service. Their influx slowly meant a takeover of duties formerly performed by ex-Southern types. (1106)

The use of 'Britannia' class 4–6–2s on former SR lines was limited, although for a while no. 70004 'William Shakespeare' was a commonly seen engine. Again the exposed wheels and mechanism are visible, while the use of just two cylinders meant reduced construction and, it was hoped, servicing costs. Those examples of the class on the Southern Region were later transferred to the LMR. (1108)

A Portsmouth–Southampton line working, still with LSWR stock but 'Standard' no. 76012 at the head. The location is Portsbridge Junction and the date 3 May 1953. (1117)

Push-pull working on a Stephenson Locomotive Society special at Fareham in May 1953. The engine, no. 30110, appears to have been specially cleaned for the duty and is seen here having its tanks replenished before departure towards Eastleigh via the tunnel avoiding line. (1120)

'Standard' Class 3 tank no. 82015 at Eastleigh in May 1953, again heralding the departure of former LSWR and LBSCR types to the scrapyard. Powerful and free steaming, the engines also possessed a well-protected cab, although these could become very hot in the summer. (1123)

On Sunday 17 May 1953 the Railway Correspondence & Travel Society organised a rail tour of Southampton Docks and Fawley, with the requested motive power no. 30757 'Earl of Mount Edgcumbe'. The engine at that time was based at Plymouth but an obliging railway had it worked especially to Eastleigh, where it is seen just before the start of the tour. (1128)

No. 30757 worked the special of five coaches and a van to Fawley, where USA tank no. 30062 took over for the remainder of the tour. The latter is seen here working hard near Totton and bound for the docks. (1132)

First signs of change and one of the pioneering LMS twins, no. 10000 at Southampton Central on 1 August 1953. Along with sister engine no. 10001, no. 10000 spent some time on the former South Western lines around this time and with one of its regular turns the 'Royal Wessex' express. Power was similar to a 'West Country' worked hard, although this could be achieved by the turn of a tap – even if drivers were never sure if opening the controller would result in movement or a flash and cloud of smoke! (1170)

'L1' class 4–4–0 no. 31788 alongside the Eastleigh coaling stage in July 1953. At the time this engine was still principally working on its home territory of former SECR lines, although following electrification there in 1957 a number of the class were transferred to either Nine Elms or Fratton. Despite being basically good engines they were never popular on the South Western division, partly because they had displaced familiar types and partly because of their own general rundown condition. (1166)

Not to be outdone in the face of modernisation, Bulleid was involved in the construction of three similar diesel-electric machines, nos 10201–3. Seen here at Brighton in May 1954, the engines spent some time working out of Waterloo before being drafted away to the LMR for the remainder of their lives. (1305)

No. 32328 'Hackworth' at Fareham on a coastal working in May 1953. Of the seven engines of the type this was the first to go in January 1955, after being diagnosed as having cracked frames and a weak firebox. Their duties were taken over by the 'Standard' types seen earlier. (1178)

Resting between duties, 30858 'Lord Duncan' reposes at Eastleigh in August 1953. (1185)

Another LMR 2–6–4T no. 42079 on the same day. A common sight on former LBSCR lines, the series was less seen around the Hampshire area, as the BR 80xxx series was preferred. (1186)

One of the 'Ivatt' or 'Mickey Mouse' tanks, this is no. 41293 (another LMS design) outside the shed on 15 August 1953. A number of the class were destined to spend most of their working lives on the Southern, one in particular, no. 41319, working as shunter in Eastleigh East yard almost to the very end of steam. (1187/8)

A delightful study of Adams '0395' class no. 30570 outside a very smoky shed in April 1954. The engine portrays an almost pleading look, heightened by the slight backwards slope to the smokebox. (1208)

First of the interlopers, a 350 h.p. diesel shunter. The advantage over steam was obvious: ready for work at only a few minutes' notice, cleaner and only one man required on the footplate. Forty-plus years later the same basic design persists, many examples having survived various changes to numbers and livery. No. 15230 is seen here in black at Eastleigh on 15 August 1953. (1190)

Adams '0395' class no. 30571 'out to grass' in August 1953. The survivors of the class based at Eastleigh were a common sight on light goods duties, which often involved the shunting of the numerous station yards at a time when such facilities were provided at almost every location. (1189)

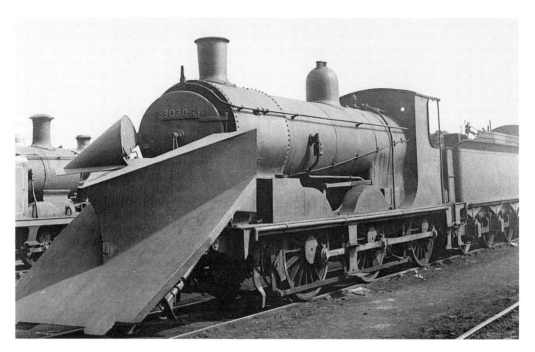

The use of snow ploughs affixed to members of the '0395' class has already been referred to; another class used for similar work was the '700' or 'Black Motor' design. Interestingly no. 30306 displays ingenuity in allowing access to the smokebox to clean out ash, etc. when a snow plough was affixed. No. 30306 was seen at Eastleigh in April 1954, no doubt due to have its appendage removed shortly. (1224)

Another example of the class, but this time fitted with an extended smokebox – as witness the overhang ahead of the front sandboxes. Principally intended for goods work, it was not unknown for the class to be pressed into passenger service at times of peak demand, although the occasions when this occurred were few and far between after the late 1930s. (108)

Wally also made the occasional visit to record steam other than on shed, an example being his view of 'C2X' no. 32541 at Bognor on 17 April 1954. The rolled up material on the cab handrail is of interest, precautions against inclement weather – or is it part of the crew's uniform? (1225)

On the same day he recorded 'E5X' no. 32570 engaged on shunting duty at Horsham. Once the junction for the steam worked cross country route from Guildford, Horsham is now pure electric. An indication of that means of traction is given by the protected conductor rails in the foreground. (1227)

Sister engine to the 'U1' depicted previously, this is no. 31904 of the class with the fireman seemingly attending to some task atop the tender. Still working Kent Coast expresses up until the time of electrification, their transfer to the Central Section meant their work was now concentrated on semi-fast and slow turns to Brighton, Redhill and Ashford, displacing in turn older LBSCR engines which were thus withdrawn. (1247)

Another of Wally's wanderings took him to Eastbourne on 30 May 1954, where 34089 '602 Squadron' is seen unusually perhaps with a West of England headcode. Possibly this was for a train destined for that area, as the duty 102 is also shown along with 'SPL' on the lower headcode disc – meaning 'special'. (1304)

Toward the West Country now, although only as far as Templecombe where 'G6' no. 30162 is seen complete with chalked star on the smokebox. This was once a feature of LSWR locomotives, although in more durable polished form. Two of the class were regularly employed yard shunting at Templecombe, where there was considerable interchange of traffic between the West of England and Somerset and Dorset routes. 5 June 1954. (1318)

Back to Sussex again and this time to St Leonards, where 'Terrier' tank no. 32670 is seen on 12 August 1956. This class was to the design of William Stroudley, and here a number of variations to the basic type can be seen. On close examination these manifest themselves on this engine with supports for elevated headcode discs above the buffers. (1348)

Having referred to the class it would not be fair if one at work on the Hayling Island branch were not included. No. 32650 has just arrived at the Terminus from Havant, with a delightful old taxi awaiting hire on the forecourt. (1329)

The three survivors of the 'Beattie' well tank design were retained for working between Bodmin and Wenford Bridge in Cornwall. Far from being at its usual home, though, no. 30587 is seen at Eastleigh apparently fresh from overhaul. Outliving their sister engines by over sixty years, the three continued to work until 1962 when they were replaced with former GWR 'Pannier Tanks', themselves displaced by diesels from duty at Weymouth Quay. (1340)

Working hard and yet with steam gushing from the safety valves, 'T9' no. 30288 rushes through Millbrook with a Bournemouth-bound working on 26 August 1954. On the extreme right the two lines afforded exit from the Western or 'New Docks', while the train itself is running on the down local line. The down 'fast' does not have a platform face. (1363)

Restored and awaiting display in the then Railway Museum at Clapham, 'Boxhill', another Brighton 'Terrier' poses outside Eastleigh in 1954. (1368/9)

Within the same line-up is the preserved Adams' flyer, or more accurately 'T3' class 4–4–0 no. 563. It was a lucky reprieve for this particular engine for it had previously been sent to Kimbridge Junction near Romsey to await breaking up, but was saved as a former LSWR engine had to be displayed at Waterloo, in as near as possible original condition. No. 563 was selected for this purpose and after the display was over it was taken to Farnham carriage sheds for storage. It was while in store that the previous exhibition finish deteriorated, and both no. 563 and 'Boxhill' are seen awaiting a further visit to the works for restoration to suitable display condition. (1368/9)

On 4 September 1956 for some reason no. 34056 'Croydon' appeared at Fratton near Portsmouth displaying the headboard for the 'Atlantic Coast Express'. No reason for this addition is reported, and it may even have been part of a practical joke by some staff. (1396)

Last rites on the Meon Valley line in 1955, with 'D1' class 4–4–0 at Privett station heading south. (G1411)

Another last trip on the Meon Valley line on 6 February 1955, when two 'T9' class engines, nos 30301 and 30732, had charge of an RCTS special heading north towards Alton on the day after passenger services had been withdrawn. (G1415)

In its new rebuilt guise, seen here at Eastleigh in 1956, 35018 'British India Line' presents a marked contrast to its previous shape. It was said drivers preferred the unmodified type while fitters preferred this version. The result, though, was arguably one of the best proportioned express classes seen in the latter days of steam. (1418)

Rebuilt 'Merchant Navy' class 4–6–2 no. 35020 'Bibby Line' leans to the curve outside Southampton Central and accelerates away towards Bournemouth with the 'Belle' in August 1956. In the background are the chimneys of Southampton Power Station, a landmark for many years: like the train they are but a distant memory. (1424)

A number of the 'Light Pacific' type were also subsequently rebuilt along similar lines to their larger cousins, although here is no. 34019 'Bideford' in original form at Worting Junction, west of Basingstoke, 4 August 1956. Worting was the point of divergence for the Bournemouth and Salisbury lines, the train passing the railwaymen's cottages at the actual junction and bound for the Salisbury route. (1421)

Having just left Northam Curve, 'Standard 4' no. 76008 passes Hartington Road as it heads towards Mount Pleasant. A little further north at St Denys the train will cross over to the right and take the Netley line to its eventual destination of Portsmouth. Interestingly the Western Region stock has roofboards affixed although it is not possible to determine their wording. (1425)

At rest at Eastleigh is another 'Standard 4', no. 75074 and the larger variant to the 76xxx series. A number of these engines were also based on the Southern and worked both semi-fast passenger, van and goods services including, for a while, oil trains from Fawley destined for Bromford Bridge. (1426)

A brace of 'M7' class 0–4–4s are seen working a service non-stop through Millbrook, 7 August 1956. Double heading was not a feature on the Region and so it is likely one of the engines was working back to its own depot. Both no. 30356 (leading) and no. 30130 are in dirty black, while the coaching stock is an LSWR set. (1428)

Easy work for 'Q1' no. 33023 at Swanwick on 9 August 1956 with a short goods. The engine is supposed to be in black, but dirty grey would perhaps be a better description – so typical of steam in its final years. (1437)

At the same location 34047 'Callington' heads west; the first four vehicles are BR 'Mark 1' type. The centre vehicle of the line-up is of interest, appearing to be at a somewhat drunken angle; yet no heads appear out of the train and even under a glass it is not possible to determine if anything is amiss. (1438)

Approaching Swanwick, this time from the direction of Netley, is no. 31793 with what is mainly Maunsell stock. Visible above the roofs of the train is the home signal affording entry to the station, which was a lower doll owing to sighting requirements. (1441)

Fareham on 9 August 1956; no. 75079 is awaiting departure for Portsmouth at the head of Bulleid stock. Fareham was also the junction for the original line to Gosport, although this closed to passengers as early as 1953. On the extreme right the chimneys of the original station building can be seen. It was said that in the earliest days of the railway a bell was hung in the space between and was rung to indicate the impending departure of a service. (1446)

Another BR Standard type in the form of 73116 leaving Fareham for Southampton in October 1962, this time with what appears to be Midland Region stock behind the tender – possibly a diverted service. This was one of several of the class working on the Southern to carry the same name as formerly bestowed on one of the early series 'King Arthurs' – the same name but not the same name-plates: a pleasing gesture in the closing years of steam traction. (3532)

Returning now for a final look at steam at Eastleigh, commencing with a beautifully clean 'M7' no. 30034 fresh from overhaul, and in decided contrast to its Brighton stablemate. The photograph was taken on 18 August 1957. (1456)

Another engine fresh from the works, but this time on 8 September 1957, was no. 30337. Despite its seemingly pristine condition this was its swansong, for no. 30337 would survive just a further fifteen months in service, ending its days in December 1958 – the same year that six others of the class were also condemned. (1460)

Maunsell series 'King Arthur' no. 30790 'Sir Villiars', also in September 1957. This time the later series BR emblem is carried affixed to the side of a large capacity bogie tender, of the type several of the class ran with. (1461)

A mainland 'O2', no. 30223, at Eastleigh on 8 September 1957, complete with what appear to be storm sheets above the cab. A bucket and shovel also lie across the tank top, the former at a precarious angle; it is hoped its position was noted before the engine was next moved. (1464)

To conclude the scene at Eastleigh, this is no. 80137, a 'Standard Class 4' tank engine in August 1962; this really typified the designs built from 1950 onwards. No frills, just functional, powerful and reliable – and yet a number would have a life of less than ten years, foreshortened by electrification and the need to abolish steam almost, it seemed, at any cost. (3407)

No excuses for having used this view in a previous book, as Bulleid's diesel shunting design was a unique and somehow attractive design. It is seen here at Norwood Junction with the standard Bulleid wheels. Despite its reasonable reliability the design was not proceeded with further and like the steam engines produced by him, the last Chief Mechanical Engineer of the Southern, its place is in the history books.

Other titles available from The History Press

Durham Railways

CHARLIE EMETT

Ever since the Stockton & Darlington Railway opened in 1825 the north-east of England has been at the heart of the railway system. Charlie Emett, ex-railwayman, author and historian, has collected a fascinating selection of over 250 photographs, all informatively captioned. His compilation takes the reader on a journey from these pioneering beginnings, through the revolutionary age of steam and the diesel era, to the birth of the electric expresses, drawn by the most powerful locomotives ever to run in Britain.

978-0752449555

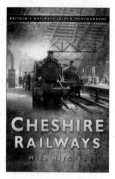

Cheshire Railways

MIKE HITCHES

Cheshire Railways is a detailed insight into the branch lines of Cheshire. Mike Hitches provides us with a rich pictorial history, highlighting the golden age of steam, through to the sad closure of many of the county's lines in the 20th century. Crewe is one of the most famous places for railway history, as it was home to London & North Western's railway workshops and a major junction on the West Coast main line. *Cheshire Railways* includes the fascinating history of Crewe, at the heart of Cheshire's railway system. This book will delight rail enthusiasts and fascinate those who are interested in this key part of Cheshire's history.

978-0752449791

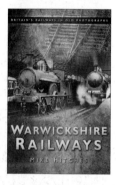

Warwickshire Railways

MIKE HITCHES

Warwickshire Railways is a fascinating account of the changes and developments which particularly characterized this stretch of railway. Archive photographs, some never before seen, period timetables, company advertisements and loco-shed allocations also add to the atmosphere and vividly conjure up a picture of a mode of transport that has, sadly, long gone. This nostalgic collection will appeal to train enthusiasts, local historians and the general public alike and is an essential guide to an important part of our railway heritage.

978-0752449333

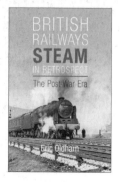

British Railways: Steam in Retrospect

ERIC OLDHAM

In 1948, the 'big four' railway companies were nationalized to form British Railways. This collection of photographs captures the last two decades of steam power as steam gave way to diesel electrification, including many vintage locomotives of pre-Grouping origin that survived the war plus the final steam locomotive to be built on British Railways. In particular, Eric Oldham looks at Crewe and Doncaster stations/works, MPDs in general, along with steam on the Woodhead route, pre/post electrification The photographs include behind-the-scenes views of locomotive sheds, depots, freight and passenger traffic plus some dramatic station portraits.

978-0752450186

If you are interested in purchasing other books published by The History Press, or in case you have difficulty finding any History Press books in your local bookshop, you can also place orders directly through our website

www.thehistorypress.co.uk